Unfading Beauty

"A blessed book! This is a very good teaching and much needed in the Body of Christ. My Sister in Christ, Dr. Karen Ranney speaks volumes of big truth in this one little book. She backs it all up with God's uncompromised Word and somehow wraps it all in His incredible love for humanity.

"I was not surprised she wrote on this subject so well, as I have watched her and her husband embrace God's love and walk in His Truth; as well as, teach and demonstrate them to others everywhere they travel.

"I believe: we've not yet seen this wonderful couples' teaching ministry in full manifestation—but it's coming."

Aaron D. Jones, Author of 8 books
Christian Publisher
Evangelist and Missionary

Dr. Karen Y. Ranney

Unfading Beauty

HOLY BIBLE
KING JAMES VERSION

Volume I
Today's Proverb 31 Woman Series

Christian Literature & Artwork
A BOLD TRUTH Publication

Unfading Beauty (Vol. 1)
Copyright © 2020 Karen Y. Ranney
ISBN 13: 978-1-949993-66-0

Today's Proverbs 31 Woman (series)
FIRST EDITION

Jew and Gentile Ministries
P.O. Box 1981 ▪ Sapulpa, OK 74066
www.jewandgentileministries.org

BOLD TRUTH PUBLISHING
Christian Literature & Artwork
606 W. 41st Street, Ste. 4 ▪ Sand Springs, OK. 74063
www.BoldTruthPublishing.com
boldtruthbooks@yahoo.com

Available from Amazon.com and other retail outlets. Orders
by U.S. trade bookstores and wholesalers.

Quantity sales special discounts are available on quantity
purchases by corporations, associations, and others. For
details, contact the publisher at the address above.

10 20   Printed in the USA.   10 9 8 7 6 5 4 3 2 1

Dedication

This book would never have been written without the Holy Spirit prompting me so strongly. I praise God for giving me this opportunity to share my heart and His heart with women. My main inspiration has come from my precious mother, Elwanda McMinn. Mom taught me the Word of God as a child and led by her example of a godly, holy life. She is a prayer warrior and has shared with me, through prayer and counsel, in the making of this book. Thank you, mom!

My husband, Allen Ranney, has also been a great inspiration in the writing of this book. He has been a sounding board for my thoughts, that have sometimes been quite lengthy…bless his dear heart for his encouragement and patience in helping me in the writing of this book.

Table of Contents

Contents

Foreword

When I first heard, my wife, Karen speaking about how her heart ached for women because of the lies they've been spoon fed since they were babies I had to stop and ask her what she was talking about. Karen then began to explain that because women do not know God's love and affirmation of them, society, with its ever-changing standards has done a great disservice to women all over the world, especially in the western world, Europe and America.

Imposing on them immoral standards of dress, speech and behavior under the guise of progressive modern thinking.

Deceiving them to believe that the new best thing, the "fad" or "rage" in clothing style is to expose more and more of yourself. Modesty being thrown out the window as antiquated. Chastity, purity, holiness and righteousness mocked by an ever-increasing sinful culture.

I asked what could be done? What should be done?

Karen explained that she had a book in her heart about how God wants to have a close love relationship with women which will cause them (by showing them His love, affirmation and acceptance) to want to please the Lord with godly standards. I thought wow! If there is a lady qualified to write that book it would be Karen, as she was raised with sound biblical teaching, her father being a pastor, and she has a personal, close relationship with Jesus and loves to read/study the Word of God.

Karen lays a firm scriptural foundation for every statement in this book and by the time you finish reading, you will understand she is that Proverbs 31 woman and you are well on your way to become the next.

Brace yourself and prepare your heart, mind and spirit to receive what God is telling women about His desire for an intimate relationship with them and how this will affect how they act, dress and speak.

> Proverbs 12:4
> *"A virtuous woman is a crown to her husband: but she that makes ashamed is as rottenness in his bones."*

Shalom,

Dr. allen Ranney

Allen C. Ranney, Th.D

Author's Preface

The reason this book is being written is I have felt compelled by God, as a Christian woman, to care for other women's needs and concerns. This has been on my heart for quite some time. Because of struggles in my own life, as a woman, my heart goes out to women who struggle with low self-esteem, tormenting thoughts, lack of real peace, feeling in competition and comparison with other women. This has caused me to cry out to God and to study His Word in regards to the needs of women everywhere. God's heart breaks and so does mine with how the enemy of our souls has brought such torment into our hearts that does not have to be there.

In the book of Titus 2:3-5 it says "The aged women likewise, that they be in behavior as becomes holiness, not false accusers, not given to much wine, teachers of good things; "That they may teach the young women to be sober, to love their husbands, to love their children, "To be discreet, chaste, keepers at home, good, obedient to their own husbands, that the Word of God be not blasphemed."

I may not be an aged woman, at least I hope I don't look like one, ha, ha, but I have been a Christian since I was a girl, nine years old, about 50 years. I have struggled in many of the areas that I would like to address in this book. My heart goes out to women everywhere who struggle in these same areas. Even though I was raised as a Pastor's kid and heard and learned many things from the Bible, I still struggled with understanding how much God loves me and how precious and beautiful I am in His eyes. It seems like I could not understand the will of God for my life as a Christian woman. I struggled with being able to rightly divide the Word. I also struggled with trying to understand what was legalism or what was pleasing to God.

I'm sure that there are many women who will read this that have the same or similar struggles. Since God has given me more understanding of the whole picture in the last few years and what His heart is, I would like to share this with as many women as possible. If I can help even one woman not to struggle the way I have in my life it will be worth it all. After much prayer and contemplation seeking the Lord's face, this is what I believe He wants me to share from His Word and His heart. I pray it will be a very encouraging exhortation and a help to each and every one that reads it.

In Christ,

Dr. Karen Ranney

Karen Y. Ranney, Th.D

Introduction

I have enjoyed writing this book knowing that my Heavenly Father delighted in downloading this into my heart to share with my dear sisters in Christ.

We, as women, seem to have an insatiable desire to be beautiful. I know, I have. It seems to drive us and cause us to be discontent, always searching for affirmation, praise, and even love from others. The world comes to us in our weakness and torments us with causing us to conform to others and their opinions.

My struggle in understanding God's love and acceptance of me has caused me to want to help my sisters in Christ find this freedom that only a close relationship with Jesus can bring.

What issues are you, dear sister, struggling with in your life? Are you searching for an everlasting love, true affirmation and/or praise that will build you up and make you whole?

This book is about helping us to see Jesus' face and to understand His deep, everlasting love, gentleness, tender mercies, and loving kindness to us as women. It is to help us seek Christ's face and to know His great love that desires us to be made whole in Him. To know the Love of Christ that surpasses all understanding. To know His perfect love that casts out all fear. To be set free to live in abundant love, peace and joy.

Do you desire an intimate, close relationship with Jesus that causes you to desire with all your heart to please Him and be His bride, or do you want to desire it? If so then you will enjoy reading this book.

My heart prayer is that every woman who reads this book will find the love of Jesus Christ that will liberate her soul and bring a wholeness and intimate relationship with Him that will saturate her spirit and soul with "Unfading Beauty".

Song

Let the Beauty of Jesus Be Seen In Me

Let the beauty of Jesus be seen in me,
All His wonderful passion and purity.
May His Spirit divine, all my nature refine,
Let the beauty of Jesus be seen in me.
When your burden is heavy and hard to bear
When your neighbors refuse all your load to share
When you're feeling so blue,
don't know just what to do
Let the beauty of Jesus be seen in you.
When somebody has been so unkind to you,
Some word spoken that pierces you
through and through.
Think how He was beguiled, spat upon and reviled,
Let the beauty of Jesus be seen in you
From the dawn of the morning till close of day,
In example in deeds and in all you say,
Lay your gifts at His feet, ever strive to keep sweet
Let the beauty of Jesus be seen in you.

Author: Albert Orsborn

"Favor is deceitful, and beauty is vain: but a woman that feareth the Lord, she shall be praised."

– Proverbs 31:30

"And let the beauty of the Lord our God be upon us..." – Psalm 90:17a

Chapter One
Unfading Beauty

*H*ave you, as a woman, ever just wanted to be beautiful? Do you strive to make yourself beautiful? I will be the first to admit, I have, almost obsessively. But, have I ever felt like I attained it? No absolutely not, it is quite fleeting.

What is your definition of beauty? What is the world's definition of beauty? Are they the same? Why do we as women, have such a strong desire to be considered beautiful? Why are we driven by this passion?

Do you think that maybe we are driven by this passion because we are looking for affirmation, attention, love, and we feel in competition or compared with other women? There is a lot of competition between women, especially in the world. When I say world, I am talking about most women, because even we, who are Christians, have a tendency to feel the competition and comparison. It is a driving force in our lives and causes us to feel like we need to conform to other women's ideals so we will be accepted or even thought of as "better than others".

Why do we as woman feel such pressure to compete with other women? I believe most of it is because we are so inundated in our society with "beauty" and "comparison". We are saturated with it in all directions. This is too bad because it affects everything we do and causes us not to look to God for our affirmation and love, but to others, which always frustrates and never satisfies.

Maybe you would say, "I'm not frustrated". Honestly, let's think about how our society is so inundated with what they call beauty. Let's see, we have beauty salons, beauty schools, beauty departments in stores, beauty magazines, books about the "how to" of beauty, commercials about beauty, etc.

Some women actually are so obsessed with beauty, they abuse their bodies to attain this fleeting attribute. Examples: Diets leading to anorexia and bulimia, face-lifts, dermabrasions and surgeries. Some women, do all kinds of things that are uncomfortable or unhealthy (like high heels, putting up with the chemical stench

Unfading Beauty

of ammonias/dyes, nail care products and sun burning/tanning) not realizing that worldly beauty standards are very elusive even impossible to obtain. Why do we torture ourselves trying to be beautiful and stay that way? Do you ever ask yourself this question? We should. I am asking myself this question.

Do you realize how much money and time is spent chasing after the elusive dream of worldly beauty? New research on the New York Post website says that Groupon's study celebrated the official start of summer by asking 2000 American women the amount of money they spend on their appearance and uncovered some interesting trends.

The women surveyed who said they routinely spend money on their appearance spend an average of $3,756 a year ($313 a month), which adds up to $225,360 throughout their entire lifetime (ages 18-78). Would you say this is an astronomical amount? You could buy a very nice house with that much money or go on several worldwide trips. When I began to think about how much money I have spent, it made me feel like I had wasted a lot of money.

Then we must ask the question…how does God feel

about all of this? Is this insatiable desire to be beautiful what God intended for us as women? Does He really want us to be driven by this beast? Driven by lust to be something more than we are? Driven by what others think about us? Driven by this ferocious beast that never lets up…that never gives us a break…that never stops eating at us? I have to be honest that most of my life I have suffered from this torturous never-ending struggle without peace or satisfaction. Why? Why do we as women feel like we can never be good enough, or look as good as other women? I have found that no matter how perfect I try to be I never feel quite good enough. Do you have these feelings?

Why do we, as women, allow ourselves to be so trapped, so driven, so imprisoned, so captive to this lust for worldly beauty? Why does it rule and reign in our lives? Why has it taken me all these years to see the deception of it…and the slavery?

Why have we as women, godly women, not searched out the Word of God to see what God has to say about this monster? Well, I believe it is time for us women to make war against this beast. I pray we can come to the place where we can say that we are "content (satisfied) in whatever state we are in" (Philippians 4:11)…we can

Unfading Beauty

know the "peace which passes understanding" (Philippians 4:7) and we can know the "fullness of the love of God" which will cast out all fear. (1 John 4:18)

Notes:

Notes:

"Turn away mine eyes from beholding vanity; and quicken me in thy way." – Psalm 119:37

 Chapter Two
Vanity, Vanity

I have most definitely had a fear of man (or woman) …in what they think of me. But we need to have the "fear of God". In Proverbs 31:30, we see that "Favor (charm) is deceitful and beauty is vain (passing) but a woman that <u>feareth the Lord</u> she shall be praised".

Is this our motive for wanting to be beautiful (worldly beauty); to be praised? I must honestly say, "For many it is and has been a motive". But we must ask ourselves? Does it bring peace, joy and love to our lives? It most definitely has not mine. Whatever pleasure I have gotten from the praise of men and women has been fleeting… I always needed a new dress, a new pair of shoes, a new purse, etc., so I could receive some kind of praise.

Why is it we crave other's attention? Why does the "fear of man" bring a snare to our soul?

Unfading Beauty

This was brought to my attention when I married my husband. He seemed to love me just the way I was every day. I never had been happy with myself no matter how I looked. I always could find fault with myself...I guess being a perfectionist did not help. His acceptance and even admiration of me was there whether I was all dressed up with makeup and pretty clothes or I had just gotten out of the bed with unkempt hair. It blew me away.

I began to realize I had been fed a lie all my life, or had believed a lie. Where did this lie come from? Why did he think I was beautiful, even gorgeous, with not even a dab of makeup or my hair fixed special? I noticed that the happier I was and the more I genuinely smiled the more he praised me. He seemed to truly believe I was beautiful. Wow! What a revelation of God's love for me to realize I am accepted and loved just the way He made me!

Have you ever seen women all decked out with strikingly beautiful clothing, lots of precise makeup, nails manicured/pedicured, and lots of pretty jewelry but with a sour expression? What was your thoughts or impressions? Did you have thoughts of how beautiful they were? Were you impressed with all of their outward statements of so-called beauty? Well, I know what I have thought. It did not matter to me what kind of

Vanity, Vanity

fashion or beauty statement they were making, I did not think of them as beautiful. (1 Peter 1:14)

What are your thoughts when you see a woman, with no makeup, no fancy clothes, no well-coiffed hair, and no jewelry, but with a great big smile, a sweet gentle spirit, and kind compassionate eyes full of love? Oh, and also a beautiful shine on her face from Jesus' presence in her life? I have admired women who have had these true beauty qualities. Have you?

Why does this world, especially in America, make us feel like we have to conform to a certain mold? Why do we as Christian women fall into the trap of conforming to this world's mold? (cf: Romans 12:1-2)

Conformity always brings to my mind, being molded into a tight box, keeping us in a prison to the ways of man. It makes me feel like I can't really be myself, or be free to be me. It always introduces itself as an enjoyable play thing but it becomes a bondage that never let's go its grip on our souls. It looks like a very inviting, exciting room to play around in but later we realize it is actually a dismal prison, that cuts off our souls from the light and love. It binds us to "other's opinions" rather than the freedom that comes from God's acceptance and love.

Notes:

"Honour and majesty are before Him: strength and <u>beauty are in His sanctuary.</u>" – Psalm 96:6

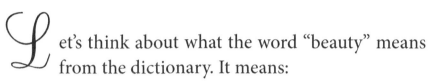

Chapter Three
Ageless Beauty Treatments

*L*et's think about what the word "beauty" means from the dictionary. It means:

1. Giving pleasure to the mind or senses.
2. Giving the greatest pleasure and stirring emotions.
3. A person's physical features are considered aesthetically pleasing.
4. A particularly graceful, ornamental, or excellent quality.

I like #4. It says "A particularly graceful, ornamental, or excellent quality". Does God love beauty? Yes! Then, we have the question does God want us to be beautiful? Yes! Well the only way to learn more about these questions is to go where God speaks to us, the Bible. When I started really delving into the study of true beauty in the Bible and other books, I began to realize that, hey,

Unfading Beauty

God IS into women being beautiful, BUT what are His thoughts about it? Maybe we should back up and see if we want to please God, ourselves or other people? Or are we triple minded? Ha-ha! Can we be triple minded and please God?

Well, that is what this book is about. Let's allow God's Holy Spirit, to check out our hearts. First of all, do we really know God, Jesus His Son, in our heart of hearts? Have we truly had a born again, repentant heart, that has been transformed by the light of Christ's love and glory? Let's look at how this can happen in our lives.

> *Acts 2:37*
> *"Now when they heard this, they were pricked in their heart, and said unto Peter and to the rest of the apostles, Men and brethren, what shall we do?*

(They were asking what they must do to be saved, born again, converted) Peter answered in verse 38:

> *"Then Peter said unto them, Repent, and be baptized every one of you in the name of Jesus Christ for the remission of sins, and ye shall receive the gift of the Holy Ghost."*

Ageless Beauty Treatments

Of course, if we have never had a truly born-again experience with Christ changing our hearts then we will have strong desires to fulfill the lust of our flesh man (woman). But I trust that each of the women who read this book have a heart that is born again and desire to please God (or will cry out to God for this heart) above all others, even yourself.

Then if we have truly let Christ into our hearts and minds, let us go on to learning how to be beautiful in His sight. Do we truly have a passionate desire to please and make our Lord and Savior happy with us? This is so deep because it entails so very many aspects of us as women.

I will try to share from my heart and experience over the years, how God has been so patient, kind, loving, merciful and faithful to speak intimately to me concerning my relationship with Him as a daughter and also as the Bride of Christ. God's loving kindness, tender mercies and His extravagant love are one of the most precious, valuable life-changing, face lifting, beauty treatments of all times. This kind of beauty is ageless, eternal, fades not away, is wrinkle free, lasting, attractive, desirable, pure, holy, and praised by God.

Why does man (woman) kind always try to invent or

make up their own ways of being good and bringing pleasure to themselves? God's ways and thoughts are so much higher than ours.

> *Isaiah 55:8*
> *"For my thoughts are not your thoughts, neither are your ways my ways, saith the Lord."*

We see in Psalm 24:3-6...

> 3 *"Who shall ascend into the hill of the Lord?*
> *Or who shall stand in His holy place?*
> 4 *He that hath clean hands, and a pure heart;*
> *who hath not lifted up his soul unto <u>vanity</u>, nor sworn deceitfully.*
> 5 *He shall receive the blessing from the Lord, and righteousness from the God of his salvation.*
> 6 *This is the generation of them that seek Him, that <u>seek thy face</u>, O Jacob. Selah"*

As we read about the children of Israel, in the Old testament and the New, mankind has, even from the beginning, been rebellious. We have thought, I say thought, because it is a myth, that we can be happy and have peace by going our own way in disobedience. If we truly want God to be our Father and be the beautiful Bride

Ageless Beauty Treatments

of Christ, then we must submit to His love.

In love He will chasten us and scourge us as a Father, showing His compassion and help us find the lowliness of heart and meekness to accept that we can never please Him in our own selves. If we, as women, will let the Holy Spirit humble us and realize that we are very needy of Jesus Christ, He can shine the light of His love, grace, and mercy towards us in the form of healing for our souls. We will find that we become joyful, happy, content, peaceful, fulfilled and beautiful… all attributes shining from our inner being of Christ's amazing grace.

Studying the Bible about true unfading beauty which comes from God's majestic, radiating, unadulterated, pure, lovely, sweet, passionate, self-sacrificing, humble Spirit, is an eye-opening, life-changing, deeply soul renovating, beauty treatment.

You may ask, "is God interested in beauty treatments for women?" You better believe He is! And His beauty treatments are so much better, lasting, and truly have much more beautiful results than woman's earthly, vain, corruptible, deceitful, frustrating, costly, lustful, discontented, selfish, striving and Holy Spirit quench-

19

Unfading Beauty

ing way of trying to become beautiful!

> *Psalm 96:6*
> *"Honor and majesty are before Him: strength and <u>beauty are in His sanctuary.</u>"*

What do you think, women? Are you finding true unfading <u>beauty</u> in God's sanctuary?

Notes:

Notes:

Notes:

"But we all, with open face beholding as in <u>a glass the glory of the Lord,</u> are changed into the same image from glory to glory, even as by the Spirit of the Lord." – 2 Corinthians 3:18

 ## *Chapter Four*
Transforming Beauty

*J*n this book I want to encourage us, as women, to find Christ's genuine beauty through a close intimate relationship with Him. This is not about rules or legalistic ways, it is about "knowing" Christ in a way that will transform us, as women, into the beautiful creatures He made us to be. God is not against us wanting to be adorned or putting on ornaments for beauty, (He made us to desire to be beautiful, desire to be praised), but what kind of ornaments are we putting on?

It is not so much about DO NOTS but about finding a more excellent way. The enemy of our souls wants to sell us on something cheap, unfulfilling, never satisfying, and frustrating. BUT GOD wants us to walk in His ways, the more excellent way.

Proverbs 3:5
"Trust in the Lord with all thine heart and lean

Unfading Beauty

not unto thine own understanding."

Psalms 93:5b, (NKJV) "Holiness adorns Your house, O Lord forever.". Are we not the house (temple) of the Lord (Holy Spirit)? May we be adorned with God's Holiness…that's true unfading beauty.

When I think about transformation, immediately my mind goes to a butterfly's metamorphosis. Why did God make a butterfly to be transformed from an egg, to larva (caterpillar), to pupa then to an adult butterfly? It is a rapidly changing process that is phenomenal and shows God's almighty, intricate detail, and wisdom. Why do we as humans want to do things different than God planned them? Why are we foolish and vain? God has made all things according to His infinite wisdom.

Why does man, who has a finite understanding, think His ways are better than Gods?

If we want to please God and be the Bride of Christ, (this is our goal, right?) should we not seek out God's way and wisdom so we will live a fruitful, faithful, fulfilling and praiseworthy life instead of a vain, wasteful, regretful, non-productive, selfish, corruptible and unfulfilling life?

Transforming Beauty

As the butterfly instinctively does what God created it to do, shouldn't we as His creatures, made in His image, be transformed into the beautiful creatures He intended for us to be, by submitting to His design and plan. I think so.

Then we come to the question, we, as women, should ask. How does God want to transform us into His glory and image? How does He want to make us beautiful in His sight for His pleasure and purposes and our own benefit?

What is so wonderful about this glorious transformation by Almighty God, maker of the Universe and Creation, is the fact that it is not just for God to show us off as His precious beautiful treasure, He also does it for our profit, that we may be a partaker of His divine nature and holiness.

Hebrews 12:10-11
10 "For they verily for a few days chasten us after their own pleasure; but He for our profit, that we might be partakers of His <u>*Holiness*</u>*.*
11 Now no chastening for the present seems to be joyous, but grievous: nevertheless, afterward it yields the peaceable fruit of righteousness unto them which are exercised thereby."

Unfading Beauty

God does this so we can live in unspeakable joy, peace that passes understanding, and amazing love that has no end.

In 2 Chronicles 20:21, God instructed the children of Israel to "worship the Lord in the beauty of Holiness". As they did God fought the battles and enemy, causing the enemies to kill their own selves, thus giving Israel rest from their enemies, great joy and prosperity. (They kept the spoil of their enemies).

When we come to the place that we truly understand we find everything in Christ…our joy, happiness, peace, love, beauty, fulfillment, and completion, we experience the greatest joy and rest that we as women could ever know. The vain fading ways of the world are a caricature of the real beauty of God's kingdom and glory. God's ways are the opposite of man's ways. Man looks on the outward appearance but God <u>looks on the heart.</u>

> *1 Samuel 16:7*
> *"But the Lord said unto Samuel, look not on his countenance, or on the height of his stature; because I have refused him: for the Lord sees not as man sees it; for man looks on the outward appearance, but the Lord looks at the heart."*

Transforming Beauty

This world we live in tells us lies but if we look into God's Word, we see the opposite.

2 Corinthians 3:17-18
17 "Now the Lord is that Spirit; and where the Spirit of the Lord is, there is liberty.
18 But we all, with open face beholding as in a glass the glory of the Lord, are changed into the same image from glory to glory, even as by the Spirit of the Lord."

I have found in my own life and as I behold the glory of the Lord as in a (mirror) glass that the beauty of the Lord shines out of my countenance causing His beauty to be seen.

From the song at the beginning of this book there are words that say: "Let the beauty of Jesus be seen and me, all His wonderful passion and purity, oh now spirit divine, all my nature refined, Till the beauty of Jesus be seen in me".

There is absolutely no comparison to the beautiful transformation that we find in the presence of the Lord compared to the so-called beauty of the world. As I have spent time worshiping and praising the Lord and

Unfading Beauty

studying His word to find out how precious and what a treasure I am to Him, I have found a joy and love that this world knows nothing about. This brings the true beauty of God on our countenance and reflects His glory. We find in Proverbs 31 that this kind of woman who fears God will be praised. It is a result of us, as women, finding our beauty in the Lord.

In Proverbs 31 verse 10, it begins asking the question, "Who can find a virtuous woman? It seems to be very important. Then it tells us her price is far above rubies.

> *Proverbs 31:30*
> *"Favour is deceitful, and (worldly) beauty is vain: but a woman that feareth the Lord she shall be praised."*

Earlier I mentioned that as women, for the most part, we try to be beautiful so we can be praised. Well, this makes it clear how we will be praised.

Do we want to be a vain person who regrets how we lived our lives? Or do we want to be a virtuous woman who is praised by her husband, children and by God?

Notes:

Notes:

"Whose adorning let it not be that outward adorning...But let it be the hidden man of the heart...the ornament of a meek and quiet spirit, which is in the sight of God of great price."

– 1 Peter 3:3-4

Chapter Five
Adorning Beauty

We read about Sarah in 1 Peter 3:3-4.

3 "Whose adorning let it <u>not be that outward adorning</u> of plaiting the hair, and of wearing of gold, or are putting on about apparel;
4 But let it be the hidden man of the heart, and that which is <u>not corruptible,</u> even the <u>ornament of a meek and quiet spirit</u>, which is in the sight of God of great price."

I'm sure she was like every other woman who has been born, having a built-in desire (human nature) to be adorned with ornaments showing her beauty to the world. BUT she had the wisdom, (did not have the Bible like we do) to realize where her true beauty came from. I believe Sarah had learned to "know God intimately", to spend time with God in His beauty and grace so she could reflect it to the world. She came to the understanding that to shine with God's true beauty she needed to submit to God's grace, showing this by trusting in God and then being in "subjection" to her husband (verses 5-6).

I believe Sarah realized she did not need to try to impress the world or her husband that she was beautiful and she understood what Proverbs 31 tells us about the so-called beauty of the world…it is vain and favor (charm) is deceitful.

1 Peter 3:5-6 says that Sarah "trusted" in God and was not afraid with any amazement.

I believe she had come to the realization that her husband and other people would let her down but God was trustable. God would protect her and fight against her enemies. God loved and cared about her intimately and in every situation, every problem. She knew that Her God had already won the victory and she was very precious and beautiful in His sight. We can also see this for ourselves in (Romans 8:37) and (Song of Solomon 2:14)

I believe Sarah had such a close intimate relationship with God that she put on "an ornament of a meek and quiet spirit, which in the sight of God is of great price"

Adorning Beauty

on herself. (Verse 4) She had a close loving, joy filled, peaceful, fulfilling life with God and out of that came the same with her husband. Sarah cared a whole lot more about being of great price in God's eyes than in any one else's, even her husband, Abraham. I believe that because she put God first, He gave her the desires of her heart. God can give us the desires of our hearts also. (cf: Psalm 37:4; Proverbs 4:7-9)

I'm sure that Sarah, like us as women, was tempted to focus on the outward appearance but as she came to experience a close intimate relationship with God, she wanted to please Him. She could see that the outward adornment and beauty were corruptible and the "meek and quiet spirit" were everlasting, not temporal. Her, "knowing" God intimately brought great joy, peace, and love to her inner being, which caused her to radiate Christ's grace and glory, the lasting true beauty.

How about you dear woman, are you tired of seeking vainly for man's (woman's) approval, praise, accolades and "desire towards you"?

We must surrender our hearts to the lover of Heaven and earth, who knows us intimately, in the deepest part of our beings and souls, and yet loves us with a love that

Unfading Beauty

is beyond our comprehension and far beyond any love that a man can have towards us.

Our main pursuit, goal and seeking after, should be to "know Jesus Christ" in the deepest part of our beings. He will then "crown us with His beauty" that will "last eternally and will not fade" (cf: Proverbs 4:7-9 and 1 Peter 1:4)

Aren't you tired of focusing in the world's mirror and seeing your temporal fading beauty taken over by wrinkles and age spots?

Even if you are not that old yet, do you want to live with regrets that you did not see God's ways which are so much higher than our ways?

Do you want to live in pride and vanity and wish you had listened to the more glorious way?

> *2 Corinthians 3:16-18*
> *16 "Nevertheless when <u>one turns to the Lord, the veil is taken away</u>.*
> *17 Now the Lord is the Spirit; and where the Spirit of the Lord is, there is liberty.*
> *18 But we all, with <u>unveiled face</u>, beholding as in a mirror the glory of the Lord, are being*

Adorning Beauty

transformed into the same image from glory to glory, just as by the spirit of the Lord."

I love the song "Turn your eyes upon Jesus, look full in His wonderful face and the things of earth will grow strangely dim in the light of His glory and grace."

Let us begin to seek our Lord's face and be transformed by His glory and grace. Let us be enveloped in His transforming love, that will radiate from our innermost being, so we can reflect Christ's beauty to the world. This should cause others to become thirsty for what we have in Christ. Then others can find their way to Jesus, the light of the world, in this sin sick dark world. We should be salt and light like Jesus asked us to be. (See: Matthew 5:13, 16)

This is TRUE UNFADING BEAUTY! I pray that we as Christian women will no longer be deceived by the world. Romans 12:1-2 Paul says, "I beseech you therefore brethren, by the mercies of God, that you present your bodies a living sacrifice, holy, acceptable to God, which is your reasonable service. And do not be conformed to this world, but be transformed by the renewing of your mind, that you may prove what is that good and acceptable and perfect will of God."

Unfading Beauty

Remember transformed means changed, "metamorphed" like a butterfly. The beginnings of a butterfly are not beautiful but the end results are, so we as we "wait on the Lord" stay in His presence, we will be transformed by the Spirit of the Lord from glory to glory."

In the third chapter of 2 Corinthians Paul says it well:

> *2 Corinthians 3:18*
> *"But we all, with open face <u>beholding as in a glass the glory of the Lord,</u> are changed into the same image from glory to glory, even as by the Spirit of the Lord".*

Is this the mirror we are looking into? That which is eternal? The only one where we will attain real lasting beauty that will never fade or end. The only one in which we will become the beautiful bride of Christ ruling and reigning with Him.

Are our lives about ourselves? Or are we supposed to follow Christ's example of caring about souls and winning them to Jesus? Like this verse in 2 Corinthians 4:3-4 we see where our gospel can be hid to them that are lost. It says,

Adorning Beauty

"But if our gospel be hid, it is hid to them that are lost: In whom the god of this world hath blinded the minds of them which believe not, <u>lest the light of the glorious gospel of Christ</u>, who is the image of God, should shine unto them".

Do we soak ourselves in Jesus' presence and love so our faces will shine with the light of the glorious gospel? I love the next Scriptures also.

> *2 Corinthians 4:6-7*
> *6 "For God, who commanded the light to shine out of darkness, hath shined in our hearts, to give the light of the knowledge of the glory of God in the <u>face of Jesus Christ.</u>*
> *7 But we have this <u>treasure</u> in earthen vessels, that the excellency of the power may <u>be of God, and not of us."</u>*

Do we have such an intimate relationship with Christ that we radiate to the world our treasure, which is coming from our inner most being? If so, then the world will see the excellency of God in our lives. Or do we just reflect the world and its darkness back to them? Again, is our gospel hidden from those who are lost? I don't know about you but I want this treasure I have in my earthen vessel to shine forth to those who need it, so they can know the light of the knowledge of the glory of God in the face of Jesus Christ. There is no greater joy, peace or love than this. There is nothing in this world as fulfilling as this treasure we have in the face of Jesus Christ.

My encouragement to us, as women, is to seek the Lord and His face. His Word is so precious to soak our souls in daily. What a beauty treatment!

Psalm 105:2-4
2 "Sing unto Him, sing psalms unto Him; talk ye of all His wondrous works.
3 Glory ye in His Holy name: let the heart of them rejoice that seek the Lord.
4 Seek the Lord, and His strength: <u>seek His face evermore.</u>"

Psalm 147:1 NKJV
"Praise the Lord! For it is good to sing praises to our God; For it is pleasant, and <u>praise is beautiful.</u>"

Psalm 149:4 NKJV
"For the Lord takes pleasure in His people; He

Adorning Beauty

will <u>beautify the humble</u> with salvation."

Psalm 90:17 NKJV
"And <u>let the beauty of the Lord our God be upon</u>
<u>us</u>, *and establish the work of our hands for us;*
yes, establish the work of our hands."

1 Chronicles 16:9-10 NKJV
9 "Sing to Him, sing psalms to Him, talk of all
His wondrous works!
10 Glory in His holy name; let the hearts of
those <u>rejoice who seek the Lord!</u>

I encourage all women to <u>seek the Lord</u> with all your
heart!

Notes:

Notes:

"Seek the Lord and His strength, <u>seek His face continually.</u>" – 1 Chronicles 16:11

 ## *Chapter Six*
Bridal Tips

How bad do you want to be the "bride of Christ"? Have you developed a close intimate relationship with Jesus?

Most little girls dream of their wedding day and the handsome man they will marry someday but does our heart, as a woman, yearn for Christ to be our groom and come for us? We should examine our own hearts to see where they are at? Do we love the world and the things in the world? God's Word tells us that "if we love the world and the things in the world, the love of the Father is not in us".

1 John 2:15-17 NKJV
15 <u>"Do not love the world or the things</u> in the world. If anyone loves the world, the love of the Father <u>is not in him</u>.
16 For all that is in the world – the lust of the

Unfading Beauty

*flesh, the lust of the eyes, and the pride of life – is
not of the Father but is of the world.
17 And the world is passing away, and the lust of
it; but he who does the will of God abides forever."*

Do you, as the Bride of Christ, want to do the will of
God in your life in every area? Or are you being deceived by loving the world and the things in the world?

Do we realize that Christ is not coming back for those
"who love the world" and the "things in the world?" He
is coming for a bride "who hath made herself ready".

> *Revelation 19:7-8*
> *7 "Let us be glad and rejoice, and give honour
> to Him: for the marriage of the Lamb is come,
> and <u>his wife hath made herself ready</u>.
> 8 And to her was granted that she should be ar-
> rayed in fine linen, clean and white: for the <u>fine
> linen is the righteousness of the saints."</u>*

He is coming for those who "look for Him". He is coming
for a "bride without spot or wrinkle or any such thing".

> *Ephesians 5:26-27*
> *26 "That He might sanctify and cleanse it with*

Bridal Tips

the washing of water by the word,
27 That He might present it to Himself a glori-
ous church, not having spot, or wrinkle, or any
such thing; but that it should be holy and with-
out blemish."

So, shouldn't we strive to "please the Lord" in all things allowing the Holy Spirit to transform us into His glorious bride? (Romans 12:1-2) To be the bride of Jesus Christ for all eternity, reigning with Him, worshipping Him, basking in His presence, is by far better than any earthly temporary fleeting things we can attain in this life. Do you as a woman desire to please the Lord in every area of your life? When a woman is in love with a man, doesn't she desire to please him?

What is our life on this earth? The Bible says it is a vapor…like steam (James 4:14) Unless we "know Jesus" in a real intimate way, this life is vain and fruitless. Do we want to come to the end of our lives and realize that we sought after the things of this world instead of seeking to know Jesus?

How can we "find the Lord" and "love Him with all of our heart? I believe this comes from seeking God's face every day…all day.

Unfading Beauty

Psalm 105:4
"Seek the Lord, and his strength: seek his <u>face evermore.</u>"

1 Chronicles 16:11
"Seek the Lord and his strength, seek his <u>face continually.</u>"

Psalm 16:11 NKJV
"You will show me the path of life; <u>In Your presence</u> is fullness of joy; At Your right hand are pleasures forevermore."

Isaiah 61:10 NKJV
"I will greatly rejoice in the Lord, my soul shall be joyful in my God; for He has clothed me with the garments of salvation, He has covered me with the robe of righteousness, as a bridegroom decks himself with ornaments, and as a <u>bride adorns</u> herself with her jewels."

Revelation 21:2 NKJV
"Then I, John, saw the holy city, New Jerusalem, coming down out of heaven from God, prepared as a <u>bride adorned for her husband.</u>"

Bridal Tips

Finding Him is the only way we can love others as we love ourselves…if we "Know" Christ's love for us. You can't give someone else something you don't have yourself.

This is my greatest desire, to know Christ, and to make Him known to others. But I can only reflect His glory and grace, I can't do it for others. We each have to have a strong desire, stronger than all other desires, to know Christ in "…the power of His resurrection, the fellowship of His sufferings, being made conformable to His death". (Philippians 3:10).

We see the parable about the wise and foolish virgins. (Matthew 25:1-13) Both groups were looking for their groom to come back to take them with Him BUT the foolish virgins expected Him sooner and did not prepare themselves with enough oil. The wise virgins had more than enough oil to wait for the groom to come. They were NOT "just getting by", like the foolish virgins, they were inundated and saturated with the "oil of the Holy Spirit", "the oil of Joy", the "…oil that makes man's face shine". (Psalm 104:15)

So, let me ask, do you seek Him? Do you love Jesus and hunger after His righteousness? I think that our lives are the fruit of that question. (Matthew 5:6)

Notes:

*"Abide in Me, and I in you. As the branch can-
not bear fruit of itself, unless it abides in the
vine, neither can you, unless you abide in Me."*

– John 15:4 NKJV

 Chapter Seven
Beauty Rest

ow do we know if we love Jesus? We see in John
14:15, 21 NKJV it says,

(v 15)
"If you love me keep my commandments".

(v 21)
*"He who has My commandments, and keeps
them, it is he who loves Me: and he who loves
Me will be loved of My Father, and I will love
him, and will manifest Myself to him".*
(See also: John 15:10)

If you're like me and have a desire for righteousness,
you have tried to do this on your own…tried to keep
God's Commandments BUT we cannot do this ourselves. (Romans 10:2-3) These Scriptures say Israel went
about to establish their own righteousness, but did NOT

Unfading Beauty

SUBMIT themselves unto the righteousness of God. We should examine ourselves to see if we do the same thing. The ONLY way we can submit to Gods righteousness is when we learn to "abide in Christ". God's righteousness only comes from a relationship, I would dare to say, a <u>close intimate relationship with Jesus.</u>

In John 15 we see this truth,

> *John 15:4 NKJV*
> *"Abide in Me, and I in you. As the branch cannot bear fruit of itself, unless it abides in the vine; neither can you, unless you abide in Me."*

The whole chapter is about "abiding in Christ". Verse 6 says, "If a man abide not in Me, he is cast forth as a branch, and is withered; and men cast them into the fire and they are burned."

We see this passage emphasizes our desperate need to "abide in Christ" and "let His Word abide in us".

As we intimately worship Jesus and abide in His presence through His Word, we will see the fruit of obedience grow in us through His grace and mercy. We will then bear the fruit of the Spirit. Galatians 5:5 says,

Beauty Rest

"For we through the Spirit wait for the hope of righteousness by faith". Galatians 5 is about "walking in the Spirit" "not in the flesh". (Galatians 5:16-26) How can we truly "walk in the Spirit"?

I find in my own life that as I "enter into His gates with thanksgiving and into His courts with praise" (Psalm 100:4) And as I "bless the Lord at all times" and "praise the Lord continually" (Psalm 34:1) along with "pray without ceasing" (1 Thessalonians 5:17) and "be anxious for nothing but in everything by prayer and supplication" (Philippians 4:6-7) that abiding in Christ becomes a way of life which produces peace and rest in my everyday life.

I believe that God has given me an acronym for the word "Rest". It is Rejoicing Every Single Time".

In Matthew 11:28-30 it shows us Jesus heart towards us...

> 28 *"Come unto me, all you that labor and are heavy laden, and I will give you rest.*
> 29 *Take my yoke upon you, and learn of me; for I am meek and lowly in heart: and you shall find rest for your souls.*
> 30 *For my yoke is easy, and my burden is light."*

Unfading Beauty

Do you, my sister and friend, want to find this true peace and rest in Christ? True <u>unfading beauty rest</u> comes this way.

Notes:

"In like manner also, that women adorn them-selves in modest apparel, with shamefacedness and sobriety..." – 1 Timothy 2:9a

 Chapter Eight
Adornment

aking into account all the things that have been said so far, I would like to study with you the verses in 1 Timothy 2:8-9 that God, through Paul, speaks to men in verse 8 and women in verse 9.

1 Timothy 2:8-9
8 "I will therefore that men pray everywhere, lift-ing up holy hands, without wrath and doubting.
9 In like manner also, that women adorn them-selves in modest apparel, with shamefacedness and sobriety; not with broided (braided with riches) hair, or gold, or pearls, or costly array; But (which become women professing godli-ness) with good works.

In verse 8 is the instruction (command) for men to pray everywhere, lifting up holy hands, without wrath and doubting.

Unfading Beauty

That is pretty clear in its meaning but the next verse 9 tells women in like manner, to <u>adorn</u> themselves in <u>modest apparel</u>, with shamefacedness and sobriety, but (which becometh women professing godliness) with good works. Doesn't it seem that the words "like manner" would mean that it is a similar instruction as the men praying lifting holy hands?

So, for a woman to adorn herself in "modest apparel", as women professing godliness, is a similar instruction. In this day and age, we live in it seems like people do not study God's Word to see His instruction for us so we can please Him. There is definitely a trend for immodest apparel in the world and in the church. Ladies, we represent the church everywhere we go! This is grievous! Is this pleasing to God? It seems that if women are dressed so immodestly and bold that God may be saying in this passage that men will be distracted from their prayer and lifting up of <u>Holy Hands</u>!

Do we as women want to be guilty before God of causing a <u>distraction</u> for men that keeps them from "lifting up Holy hands" like this passage instructs them to do? Why would these Scriptures be connected together "as in like manner" if this was not so? Both instructions are just as important, one to men and the other to women.

Adornment

We need to study what the word "modest" means in this passage. In the Greek Strong's concordance, it uses the word (kosmios) for modest meaning well arranged, seemly, modest.

Thayer's Greek Lexicon uses the word "aidos" meaning "a sense of shame or honor, modesty, bashfulness, reverence, regard for others, and through the idea of downcast eyes."

Let me ask you, as a woman professing godliness, do you feel your apparel is pleasing to God as decent, modest, bashful, honorable, shamefaced?

Or is it indecent, immodest, lewd or not portraying a sense of shame (shamefacedness), or is it disrespecting yourself or others?

I would encourage you as a woman, if you love Jesus and want to please Him above all else that you search the Scriptures and your motives about how you adorn yourself with apparel.

The word *"lewd"* which is used in Galatians 5:19-20 (NKJV) concerning the works of the flesh in Greek is "nabluth" (5039) and means: Immodesty, shamelessness.

Unfading Beauty

(nechosheth) 5179a means: lust and harlotry.

We, as women, are inundated very much with propaganda about how to be beautiful, sensual, seductive, desirable, etc. Why are we conforming to the world? In Romans 12 Paul addresses this very well.

> *Romans 12:1-2*
> *1 I beseech you therefore, brethren, by the mercies of God, that ye present your bodies a living sacrifice, holy, <u>acceptable unto God</u>, [which is] your reasonable service.*
> *2 And <u>be not conformed to this world</u>: but be ye <u>transformed</u> by the <u>renewing of your mind</u>, that ye may prove what [is] that <u>good, and acceptable,</u> and perfect, will of God.*

Conform means to be put in a box, be restricted by a certain idea, to be squeezed into something restrictive. *Transform* means to become something brand new, to be free, unrestricted.

Why would we as women want to be conformed to the ideas, restrictions, "opinion of others morality"? Aren't we to be adorned in Jesus's likeness?

Adornment

This is what the world does to us, puts us in a mold, a trap, to be "like" the world.

God's Word transforms us to be "like" Him and His Word so we can find freedom to be the "woman He created us to be." There is joy, peace, freedom, and a sense of respect for ourselves and others when we please God in our apparel. We feel great joy that we are making our groom (Jesus Christ) happy.

What a freedom and peace that comes knowing we are being made in His image (spirit, soul and body).

> *1 Corinthians 6:18-20*
> *18 "Flee fornication.; But he that commits fornication sins against his own body.*
> *19 What? No ye not that your <u>body</u> is the temple of the Holy Ghost which is in you, which ye have of God, and <u>ye are not your own</u>?*
> *20 For ye are <u>bought with a price</u>: therefore, <u>glorify God</u> in your <u>body</u>, and in your spirit, which are God's".*

So then, we should ask ourselves, how in love with Jesus are we as women and does the way we adorn ourselves produce a life that pleases Him?

Unfading Beauty

This book is not about legalistic rules or regulations. It is about the question, "How much do you love Jesus and how much do you want to please Him in your life?"

> *John 13:34 NKJV*
> *A new commandment I give unto you, that you love one another as I have loved you, that you also love one another."*

Nothing matters, in this life we are living, if this question is not settled in our hearts. There is a Scripture that says, "it is impossible to please God without faith". Another Scripture says, "Faith without works is dead". (James 2:20)

So as mature Christian women or those who are working on their maturity, we should above all things, work on "knowing Jesus" intimately. Just like a woman who is in love with a man she plans to marry, will work on doing everything she can to please him, because she is "in love" with him. Is this your heart my sister, my friend?

If this is your heart then let's go a little further in how we can please the Lord in our lives.

I believe that God, in His Word, has gender specific

Adornment

instructions for us as women. Do you think that God planned for us as women to study the Word of God specifically addressed to men?

Or do you think that we as women should want to please the Lord and make Him happy by studying the Word of God daily to see His instructions for us, as women, His beloved?

Let us talk about some of the specific instructions that God gives us, as women, in His Word.

Again in 1 Timothy He tells us,

> *1 Timothy 2:9*
> *"<u>In like manner also</u>, that women <u>adorn</u> them-selves in <u>modest apparel,</u> with <u>shamefacedness</u> and sobriety; not with broided (braided with riches) hair, or gold, or pearls, or costly array; But (which become a woman professing godli-ness) with good works."*

It seems, like I said before, that since this is a direct instruction, specifically to us women, we should, if we love Jesus and desire to please Him with all our heart, learn what this Scripture means, then do it. The next thing is to study what this Scripture actually means.

What does the word *adorn* mean?

In the dictionary, we see that the word *adorn* means "to decorate or add beauty to, as ornaments: to make more pleasing, attractive, impressive, etc.; enhance. In the Strong's concordance we see that the word "adorn" in Greek is *"kosmeo"* meaning "to put in proper order, i. e., decorate (literally or figuratively); specially to snuff (a wick): – adorn, garnish, trim. (G 2885) We see this word used in: 1 Timothy 2:9, Titus 2:10, 1 Peter 3:5, and Revelation 21:2.

As we study these Scriptures specifically addressed to women and to us as the Bride of Christ, I pray that God gives each one of us an understanding heart, God's heart for us women.

In 1 Timothy 2:9, we see that it uses the word "modest" in regard to women "adorning themselves in modest apparel".

Now we need to find out what the word "modest" means. In the Merriam-Webster dictionary (merriam-webster.com) there are four definitions for the word.

Adornment

- 1. a. Placing a moderate estimate on one's abilities or worth. b. Neither bold nor self-assertive: tending toward diffidence.

- 2. Arising from or of a modest nature.

- 3. Observing the proprieties of dress and behavior: decent

The synonyms I found in my search for the definition of "modest" are these:

- 1. shy
- 2. bashful
- 3. diffident
- 4. coy
- 5. chaste
- 6. pure
- 7. decent

- 1. <u>Shy</u> implies a timid reserve and a shrinking from familiarity or contact with others.

- 2. <u>Bashful</u> implies a frightened or hesitant shyness characteristic of childhood and adolescence.

- 3. <u>Diffident</u> stresses a distrust of one's own ability or opinion that causes hesitation in acting or speaking.

- 4. <u>Coy</u> meaning not inclined to be forward.

- 5. <u>Chaste</u> primarily implies a refraining from acts or even thoughts or desires that are not virginal or not sanctioned by marriage vows.

- 6. <u>Pure</u> differs from chaste in implying innocence and absence of temptation rather than control of one's impulses and actions.

- 7. <u>Decent</u> meaning "free from all taint of what is lewd or salacious.

We see here that modest and decent apply to how we act and dress showing our <u>outward signs of our inward chastity or purity</u>. In the Merriam-Webster dictionary we see the definition of "chastity" and "purity" being:

1. *Chastity* means:

- 1. Abstention from unlawful sexual intercourse.
- 2. Abstention from all sexual intercourse
- 3. Purity in conduct and intention.
- 4. Restraint, simplicity and design or expression.
- 5. Personal integrity.

2. *Purity* means:

- 1. The quality or state of being morally pure.
- 2. Goodness, righteousness, virtue, decency, pro-

priety, seemliness.

- 3. Taintless
- 4. Uncontaminated
- 5. Uncorrupted
- 6. Undefiled
- 7. Unpolluted
- 8. Free from any trace of the course or indecent.
- 9. Unspotted
- 10. Unstained
- 11. Unblemished
- 12. Unsullied.
- 13. Inoffensive.

In this Scripture in 1 Timothy 2:9, Paul speaking "God's Words", tells us, as women that we can be pleasing to God by asking Him to cleanse us from anything immodest in our apparel or conduct. We see that the words "modest", "purity", "decent", "chaste", "bashful", "shy", "discreet" are very similar in their meanings.

Do we want to be like Proverbs 11:22 says? "As a jewel of gold in a swine's snout, so is a fair woman which is without discretion."

Let's go on to study the rest of this passage from 1 Timothy 2:9-11 and find out what it really means.

Unfading Beauty

We see after the words "modest apparel" that it says we should adorn ourselves with "shamefacedness". We do not hear the word "shamefacedness" being used in our modern society. Do you think this could be because it is a very foreign concept to us, especially as American women?

Let's look up the meaning for the word "shamefacedness". In the Merriam-Webster dictionary it says:

1. Showing modesty: bashful, shy.
2. Showing shame: ashamed.

Here are other definitions/synonyms of "shamefacedness".

- 1. Shy or socially timid, not liking to be noticed.
- 2. Withdrawn
- 3. Meek
- 4. Demure
- 5. Unassertive
- 6. Reserved
- 7. Self-conscious.

I also decided it would be good to look up the antonyms/opposites of "shamefacedness". Some of them are:

- 1. Sassy

Adornment

- 2. Attention seeker
- 3. Proud
- 4. Arrogant
- 5. Brazen
- 6. Brash
- 7. Immodest
- 8. Cocky
- 9. Airs and graces
- 10. Loud
- 11. Boastful
- 12. Cheeky
- 13. Impudent.

Do these descriptions and definitions sound like what women's apparel and conduct are portraying today? Again, I encourage us , as women, to ask ourselves, according to this passage in 1 Timothy 2:8-11 do we truly love Jesus and want to please Him in our lives?

To be honest, I believe we are seeing the exact opposite, even in most so-called Christian women. We may tend to want to justify our actions because we think we live in a different culture than when this passage was written. If we truly have an honest and good heart then we will love the instruction that He gave us in His Word and ask God to help us do that which is pleasing to Him.

Unfading Beauty

There is a Scripture that says God is the same yesterday today and forever. (Hebrews 13:8). His Word never changes even if men change in their customs and culture. If we think that because the culture has changed it is okay to be immodest or bold, brazen, brash and the center of attention, we better cry out to God to show us His ways of holiness and righteousness. (1 Thessalonians 4:7)

The next word in this passage I would like to study is the word "sobriety". It is not used very much in our vocabulary in today's modern world. It seems to be a word "of the past". When I looked up this word in the Merriam-Webster dictionary it says: 1. The quality or state of being sober. 2. The quality of being serious.

Here are the synonyms for it:

- 1. Ernest
- 2. Graveness
- 3. Gravity
- 4. Intentness
- 5. Serious mindedness
- 6. Seriousness
- 7. Soberness
- 8. Solemnness
- 9. Staidness.

Adornment

The antonyms/opposites are:

- 1. flightiness
- 2. Flippancy
- 3. Frivolous
- 4. Lightheartedness
- 5. Lightness
- 6. Play
- 7. Unseriousness.

"Shamefacedness" and "sobriety" are ways that we as women should adorn ourselves. Only through the help of the Holy Spirit, can we judge our self whether our apparel is portraying these godly characteristics or are they revealing the opposite?

The main motive of our heart, as women professing godliness, should be to reflect God's glory. Let me ask this question to all women, do you feel that your dress and actions show that you are an attention getter, frivolous, flippant, unserious, bold, brazen, indecent, forward, impure, lewd, and ungodly?

Do you feel that you do not portray yourself, as a woman professing godliness, but you do look and act like the world?

Unfading Beauty

I will address more concerning looking like the world later on.

Moving on in 1 Timothy 2:9 it says, … "Not with braided hair, or gold, or pearls, or costly array" … I think we can see here that this part of the passage is referring to decking ourselves out with our riches in our hair or clothing. It appears that this part of the passage is not talking about fixing our hair but what our motive is, in portraying ourselves better than others.

In verse 10, it says "But which becomes women professing godliness with good works." After looking up the word "becoming" in the Merriam-Webster dictionary it says it means 1. Suitable, fitting, especially: attractively suitable//becoming modesty, causing someone to look attractive: having a flattering or attractive effect.

Synonyms for "becoming" are:

- 1. Applicable
- 2. Appropriate.
- 3. Befitting
- 4. Proper
- 5. Suitable.

I have heard this before in some teaching concerning

Adornment

our adorning with apparel. It was said that our clothing should attract people to our face <u>NOT to our body</u>. This may be what this passage is mainly speaking about. Let me ask the question to women, "does your apparel or dress attract others to your face or to your body"?

Our faces and eyes are what reflect God's glory. People can see our spirit and soul through our eyes and faces. If we are full of joy peace and love it will be shown on our faces and in our eyes. Why would we as godly women want others, especially men, to be attracted to or look at <u>our bodies</u>? Have you ever asked yourself that question?

If we look over the history of the world since the beginning of creation, we see that before Adam and Eve sinned in the garden, they were naked and unashamed, the way God made them. But when sin was allowed to conceive and brought forth death, they went and hid themselves from God using fig leaves to cover their nakedness. They did not even realize they were naked until they had sinned. After God asked Adam where he was at, God made them animal skins to cover their nakedness.

Have you ever thought about the difference between fig leaves and animal skins?

Unfading Beauty

Which one of these covers a person's nakedness more?

And then if I may be bold enough to say or ask the question do you feel that your clothing or apparel is more like fig leaves or more like animal skins?

Why did God want mankind to be covered very well? Have you ever asked this question?

Apparently, God wanted mankind to be covered modestly so that our nakedness would not be shown to others.

As I have researched in the Bible and history, it has come to my attention that normal people wore modest and decent clothing, with the exception of harlots, people who were demonically possessed or of heathen nations.

If you have ever seen pictures or videos of people from the past up until the early 1900s, they for the most part, are clothed decently and modestly. In videos of the pioneers who crossed America, we see the women in clothing dressed from neck to toe. We also see the men dressed from neck to toe. They had long sleeve shirts on. They dressed this way even in very extreme hot weather. From what I have read, women in the past, were scandalized if even their ankle showed, especially

Adornment

in the presence of men. We need to ask ourselves the question why they had, for almost 6000 years, a conscience about themselves to cover their nakedness?

Why did this change in the early 1900s? In the early 1900s, women began to wear knee length skirts. Why did it suddenly seem okay to "bare the ankle or even leg" when in previous years it was a scandal to dress that way?

We can see, obviously, in Isaiah 47:2-3 that showing the thigh or taking off the skirts is <u>shameful</u>! It says:

> *2 "Take the millstones, and grind meal: uncover the locks, make bare the leg, uncover the thigh, pass over the rivers.*
> *3 Thy nakedness shall be uncovered, yea thy shame shall be seen: I will take vengeance, and I will not meet thee as a man."*

It shows in this passage that it is a <u>judgment from God</u> and a <u>humiliation</u>. Why do we not see this from God's perspective in this nation? Why do people look at partial/nakedness as a good thing?

The dictionary says *thigh* means 1. In human anatomy,

the thigh is the area between the hip (pelvis) and the knee.

The Scripture that comes to mind in regards to why people have compromised and allowed indecent, immodest, indiscreet, unchaste, lewd dress to inundate, even so-called Christians is 2 Timothy 3:1-5. We see that Paul wrote this,

> 1 *"This know also, that in the last days perilous times shall come.*
> 2 *For men (women) <u>shall be lovers of their own selves,</u> covetous, boasters, <u>proud,</u> blasphemers, disobedient to parents, unthankful, <u>unholy,</u>*
> 3 *Without natural affection, truce breakers, false accusers, incontinent, fierce, despisers of those that are good,*
> 4 *Traitors, <u>heady, high-minded,</u> <u>lovers of pleasures more than lovers of God;</u>*
> 5 *Having a <u>form of godliness</u>, but <u>denying the power</u> thereof: from such turn away."*

We see here that in the last days perilous times shall come. The word perilous reminds me of being on the side of a mountain barely clinging to a rock, with the wind blowing. It is very dangerous. The second verse tells us that people will be lovers of their own selves.

Adornment

If we truly are honest before God and ourselves would we think that our manner of dress and actions is loving God and other people or loving our own selves?

Would you say that young women and older women's dress nowadays portrays a heady, high-minded attitude or a demure, modest, shamefaced attitude?

We see in verse four that people will be heady and high-minded, lovers of pleasures more than lovers of God. In verse five we see that it says people will have a form of godliness, but denying the power thereof: from such turn away. This is a grief to my heart as well as other Christians when we see a form of godliness, but there is no power in so-called Christians lives to desire to live a holy, righteous, pure life and dress modestly.

Let's go down into verse 12 and 13 to see some more about how perilous it will be in the last days. Verse 12 says "yes, and all that will live godly in Christ Jesus shall suffer persecution."

It makes me wonder if we are living godly lives why we are not suffering persecution?

If we are dressing and acting just like the world, will we

suffer persecution?

In verse 13 it says, "but evil men and <u>seducers</u> shall wax worse and worse, deceiving, and being deceived." It seems to me that we do understand what evil men are but do we understand what seducers are? Let me look it up in the dictionary and see what it has to say about the word *seduce*:

- 1. To persuade to disobedience or disloyalty
- 2. To lead astray usually by persuasion or false promises
- 3. To carry out the physical seduction of and ties to sexual intercourse.
- 4. Attract.

Seducer means: (1) one that tries to get a person to give in to a desire. (by the way they dress and adorn themselves)

The synonyms for *seduce* are:

- 1. Allure
- 2. Bait
- 3. Beguile
- 4. Betray
- 5. Decoy

Adornment

- 6. Entice
- 7. Lead on
- 8. Lure
- 9. Solicit
- 10. Tempt
- 11. Inveigle

- 1. <u>Lure</u> implies a drawing into danger, evil, or difficulty through attracting and deceiving.

- 2. <u>Entice</u> suggests drawing by artful or adroit means. (The way you act).

- 3. <u>Inveigle</u> implies enticing by cajoling or flattering. (The way you talk).

- 4. <u>Decoy</u> implies a luring into entrapment by artifice. (The way you adorn yourself).

- 5. <u>Tempt</u> implies the presenting of an attraction so strong that it overcomes the restraints of conscience or better judgment.

- 6. <u>Seduce</u> implies a leading astray by persuasion or false promises.

Most women know that <u>men ARE seduced</u> by the way a woman dresses or acts. I have spoken with my husband concerning how men can be seduced (or tempted to lust) by a woman's dress or actions. He has been totally

Unfading Beauty

honest with me concerning men's struggles in this area.

The Bible says in 1 Corinthians 10:

> *1 Corinthians 10:13*
> *"No temptation has overtaken you except such as is <u>common to man</u>; but God is faithful, who will not allow you to be tempted beyond what you are able, but with the temptation will also make the way of escape, that you may be able to bear it."*

So, I can only deduct that since my husband has shared with me the temptations and thoughts that the enemy brings to him by women's immodest dress and their actions, it is a great struggle for a Christian man in the world we live in.

Why should we, as Christian women or women professing godliness, want to put a stumbling block or occasion to stumble with the temptation to be solicited or seduced in front of a Christian brother?

Is this love for God or our fellow man?

If we are honest in our hearts before God, we will have

Adornment

to say that what "most Christian women" wear today does put a stumbling block or occasion for temptation before men.

In Romans 14:7-13 we see Scriptures that tell us not to put a stumbling block in our brother's way.

> *(v 7)*
> *"<u>For none of us lives to himself,</u> and no man dies to himself. 8. For whether we live, we live unto the Lord; and whether we die, we die unto the Lord: whether we live therefore, or die, we are the Lord's.*

> *(v 12)*
> *"So then every one of us shall give account of himself to God.*

> *(v 13)*
> *Let us not therefore judge one another any-more: but judge this rather, that <u>no man put a stumbling block or an occasion to fall in his brother's way.</u>"*

If the clothing or our actions are causing a man to struggle with lust and we truly love the Lord wanting to please Him, then we should be willing to change these things out of love for God and our fellow man.

We see how serious this is in Matthew 5:28-29 NKJV, where Jesus spoke about lusting after a woman.

> *28 "But I say to you, that, whoever looks at a woman to lust for her has already committed adultery with her in his heart.*
> *29 If your right eye causes you to sin, pluck it out, and cast it from you: for it is more profitable for you that one of your members perish, than for your whole body to be cast into hell."*

Jesus was letting us know how serious it is for a woman to cause a man to lust after her and a man to give into the temptation to lust. It says in verse 28 that if a man looks at a woman to lust after her he has committed adultery with <u>her</u> in his heart. It seems that women want to blame men for lusting after them, but the truth is if a woman is dressing in a manner that is provoking or seducing (tempting) the man, it is saying that she is just as guilty as he is.

Seriously, do we as, women professing godliness, want men to look at us and lust after us, knowing that it is as

Adornment

serious as them having to pluck out their eye so they do not go to hell?

This is very serious as Jesus appealed to men and women to do whatever it takes to not cause a temptation in this area. It is as serious as going to hell or not.

True love will go out of its way to deny itself for our beloved bridegroom and for others!

Notes:

Notes:

"But put ye on the Lord Jesus Christ, and make not provision for the flesh, to fulfill the lust thereof." – Romans 13:14

Chapter Nine
Sacrificial Beauty

The Book of Romans tells us:

Romans 12:1-2 NKJV
1 "I beseech you therefore, brethren, by the mercies of God, that you present your <u>bodies</u> a living sacrifice, <u>holy</u>, acceptable to God, which is your reasonable service.
2 And <u>do not be conformed</u> to this world: but be <u>transformed</u> by the renewing of your mind, that you may prove what is that good, and acceptable, and perfect, will of God."

Should we break this Scripture down into words?

It says that Paul was beseeching, meaning begging Christians to present our bodies a living sacrifice. Meaning that our lives should be a sacrifice in all areas dress, speech and actions. Giving in to our lusts is the

Unfading Beauty

exact opposite of "presenting our bodies a living sacrifice". This Scripture does not say our spirits or souls should be a living sacrifice, it says our "bodies". This tells me that the things that we do in our bodies should be sacrificial or showing love to God or our fellow man.

We also see we should present our bodies to God "holy". We, as women professing godliness, should ask ourselves if our clothing or conduct represents "holiness" or "purity". Presenting our bodies as "holy" will then be acceptable to God and we will be in the perfect will of God.

Paul goes on to say that this is just our "reasonable service to God". In other words, it seems this passage is saying that it is just reasonable, actually not even going out of our way if we obey this. God is just "expecting us to live our lives as a living sacrifice". I can't stress enough that "sacrifice" is the exact opposite of giving in to our lusts. It is dying to our own self and desires.

Let's look at some Scriptures concerning giving in to our lusts:

> *Romans 6:12*
> *"Let not sin therefore reign in your mortal body, that you should obey it in the lusts there of."*

Sacrificial Beauty

Romans 13:14 NKJV
"But put on the Lord Jesus Christ, and make no provision for the flesh, to fulfill its lusts."

Galatians 5:16
"I say then: Walk in the Spirit, and you shall not fulfill the lust of the flesh."

Ephesians 2:3
"Among whom also we all had our conversation in times past in the lusts of our flesh, fulfilling the desires of the flesh and of the mind; and were by nature the children of wrath, even as others."

Titus 2:11-14
11 "For the grace of God that bringeth salvation hath appeared to all men,
12 Teaching us that, denying ungodliness and worldly lusts, we should live soberly, righteously, and godly in the present age,
13 Looking for that blessed hope and glorious appearing of our great God and Savior Jesus Christ,
14 Who gave Himself for us, that He might redeem us from all iniquity and purify unto Himself a peculiar people, zealous of good works."

Unfading Beauty

Continuing on in Romans 12 verse 2 we see that we are not to be "conformed to this world". Doesn't conformed to this world mean that we look just like and act just like the world?

There is another Scripture that tell us "to keep ourselves unspotted from the world".

> *James 1:27*
> *"Pure religion and undefiled before God and the*
> *Father is this, to visit the fatherless and widows*
> *in their affliction, and to keep himself <u>unspot-*
> *ted from the world."</u>*

Doesn't that sound pretty simple, keep ourselves "unspotted from the world"?

It means "that we are not able to be "spotted" as a worldly person or that we do not have "spots" that look like the world.

Let me ask you, as women professing godliness, does your dress or actions come across as "looking like the world" or being "spotted as the world"?

God is looking for a heart that is <u>"honest and good"</u> a

Sacrificial Beauty

"pure" heart. We see that Jesus Christ is looking for this type of good ground in Luke 8:15 which says

> *"But that on the good ground are they, which in an <u>honest and good heart</u>, having heard the word, keep it, and bring forth fruit with patience."*

Do you have that honest and good heart that wants to please the Lord in everything you do, body, soul and spirit?

If we plan to please the Lord, we will definitely have to ask Him for an honest and good heart. We will have to desire it more than anything else in our lives, more than pleasing ourselves and more than pleasing others. It will come with a price, the price of a living sacrifice.

In 1 Corinthians 6:18–20 NKJV tells us to "glorify God in our <u>body</u> and in our spirit, which are God's". Let's read it…

> *18 "Flee sexual immorality. Every sin that a man does is outside the body; but he that commits sexual immorality sins against his own body.*
> *19 Or do you not know that your <u>body</u> is the temple of the Holy Spirit who is in you, whom*

Unfading Beauty

you have from God, and <u>you are not your own?</u> 20 For you are bought <u>at a price</u>; therefore, <u>glorify</u> God in your <u>body</u>, and in your spirit, which are God's".

We see here that <u>our body</u> is not our own. We are bought with a price. When we think of the price that Jesus paid for our salvation doesn't it cause you to realize just how much He does love us?

What do you think that price was?

I believe the price was Jesus coming to the earth, as God in the flesh, <u>living</u> a <u>totally sacrificial life</u> not pleasing Himself but being the servant of all. He was persecuted, abandoned, beaten beyond recognition, suffering mentally, emotionally, and physically in His body, beyond what anyone has ever suffered.

<u>Our bodies</u> (not our spirits or souls) are the temple of the Holy Ghost. Wouldn't this understanding cause us to humbly present <u>our bodies</u> as a living sacrifice (Romans 12:1-2) doing everything we can to bring glory to our Savior and Lord Jesus Christ?

Notes:

Notes:

"Follow peace with all men, and <u>holiness, with-out which no man shall see the Lord:</u>"
– Hebrews 12:14

Chapter Ten
What Kind of Attire?

J believe it is very important that we as, women dress in a modest, shamefaced manner so we can please God in our lives. This is so important to God that He tells the elder women to teach the younger women.

We see this in Paul's letter to Titus.

> *Titus 2:3-5 NKJV*
> *3 "The older women likewise…teachers of good things—*
> *4 that they admonish the young women to love their husbands, to love their children,*
> *5 to be <u>discreet, chaste,</u> homemakers (keepers at home), good, obedient to their own husbands, that <u>the Word of God may not be blasphemed.</u>"*

Wow! This is so important, that the "Word of God is <u>not blasphemed</u>".

Unfading Beauty

Let us look at the words discreet and chaste…

According to Strong's Concordance <u>discreet</u> means 1. Safe (sound) in mind, i.e., <u>*self-controlled.*</u>

The dictionary says, 1. "<u>careful and circumspect</u> in one's speech or actions, especially in order to avoid offense or to gain an advantage."

Chaste in the concordance means 1. Properly clean, <u>innocent, modest,</u> perfect.

The dictionary says… 1. "abstaining from extramarital, or from all, sexual intercource." 2. "Not having <u>any sexual nature or intention</u>".

Do we want to be like the woman in Proverbs 11:22? It says "As a jewel of gold in a swine's snout, so is a fair woman which is without discretion."

Shouldn't our attire and actions reflect holiness and godliness"? We see a woman without discretion or chastity in Proverbs 7. We should consider ourselves in this. This is very serious…

Proverbs 7:1-27 is written to men, but it is also written

What Kind of Attire?

to women. Let's start with verse one, it tells men, "My son, keep My words, and treasure my commands within you… Verse five in the New King James says "That they may <u>keep you from the immoral woman</u>, from the <u>seductress</u> who flatters with her words."

This is instruction to men to seek after wisdom so that they will recognize an immoral woman as a harlot or prostitute. We notice in verse five that the woman flatters with her words. We know that men are tempted by a woman that flatters with her words.

But let's look further...

> *Proverbs 7:6-15 NKJV*
> *6 "For at the window of my house I looked through my casement,*
> *7 and beheld among the simple ones, (one without wisdom) I discerned among the youths, a young man void of understanding,*
> *8 Passing through the street near her corner; and he went the way to her house,*
> *9 In the twilight in the evening, in the black and dark night:*
> *10 And, behold, there met him a woman with the <u>attire of an harlot</u>, and subtil of heart.*
> *11 She is loud and stubborn; her feet abide not*

in her house:
12 Now is she without, now in the streets, and
lies in wait at every corner.
13 So, she caught him, and kissed him, and with
an impudent face said unto him,
14 I have peace offerings with me; this day have
I paid my vows.
15 Therefore, came I forth to meet thee, dili-
gently to seek your face, and I have found you.

In verse 21 we see "With her much fair speech she caused him to yield, with the flattering of her lips she forced him. In verse 26 we see "For she has cast down many wounded: yea, many strongmen have been slain by her. Her house is the way to hell, going down to the chambers of death."

You may be wondering why I would choose this passage for this study about women's adornment, apparel, their spirits and attitudes.

Let's look at the Scripture in verse 10 it says that there met him a woman with the "attire of an harlot".

We need to ask ourselves what the *"attire of a harlot"* is?

Don't you think that a harlot is one that seduces (tempts

What Kind of Attire?

to lust) or attracts a man towards herself?

We see this in this passage her goal was to cause the man to be so attracted and seduced by her, that he could not resist wanting her. A harlot is one that does not care about others, it is <u>all about what she wants for herself.</u> She has no love for anyone but herself. We may think, but I don't look like, act like or dress like a harlot. But are you sure?

Do you dress and act in a manner that attracts or entices men to look at or lust after your body?

I believe that it would be safe to say that a lot of women <u>DO</u> dress in a manner that causes men to have a temptation to lust/look at them. You may say, that you do not desire men to look/lust after you but God wants to get down to our heart motives. We can understand our motives by thinking about what our thoughts are and by taking note of what we are thinking.

In Proverbs 7 verse 10 it says that the harlot was <u>subtil</u> of heart. What does the word *subtil* mean? The dictionary says that it means:

- 1. Elusive
- 2. Cunning

- 3. Crafty
- 4. Shrewd.

We see the same word "subtil" used in Genesis 3:1. This Scripture is talking about the serpent (Satan) who tempted Adam and Eve. We can see why the meaning of "subtil" is cunning, crafty and shrewd. This is the way Satan tempts mankind.

But why would the word "subtil" in regard to Satan be the same word it uses in Proverbs 7:10 about the harlot? In verse 11, we see a description of her. It says, "She is loud and stubborn; her feet abide not in her house: Now is she without, now in the streets, and lies in wait at every corner."

This woman in Proverbs 7, the harlot, does not sound like a, woman professing godliness, that we see Paul instructing in 1 Timothy 2:9. She sounds like the exact opposite.

She is not shamefaced, she is not modest, she is not shy, she is not demure, she is not bashful, in her apparel or in her spirit (attitudes).

She appears to be bold, loud, forward, stubborn, im-

What Kind of Attire?

modest, indecent, lewd, not sober, subtil (crafty, cunning, and shrewd). We, as women, may not think that we are being like a harlot in our dress and attitudes but is this how we are coming across to men?

When they look at us or have interaction with us, do they perceive or see us like a harlot, having the spirit of a harlot or do they see God's Holy Spirit?

This is very serious in God's eyes as we see in Proverbs 7 verse 26-27 that the harlot has "...cast down many wounded: yes, many strongmen have been slain by her. Her house is the way to hell, going down to the chambers of death."

Do we want to be guilty of causing a man, especially Christian men, to give in to their "lust", because of our immodest, indecent, or even lewd dress?

As I said previously, Jesus said "if a man looks on a woman to lust after her he hath committed adultery <u>with her</u> in his heart". (Matthew 5:28) So, doesn't this take us back to the fact that if we, through our immodest, indecent or even lewd dress cause a man to look on us to lust, that we are guilty of the same thing that a harlot does?

Unfading Beauty

Even Jesus said that a man does not have to literally commit adultery with a woman to be guilty and send his soul to hell. He just has to give in to looking and lusting after a woman. This should cause the "fear of God" in our hearts as women. This is very plain and simple.

Again, I will ask you, as women professing godliness, do you believe that you are glorifying God in your body and in your spirit in every way you can, especially in your apparel and actions? Women can dress in modest apparel and still not glorify God in their spirit. Some women just seem to have a seductive, lustful, flirty (attention seeking) attitude toward men. This is the same thing as dressing in an immodest manner.

God wants us to be "holy and pure" in all that we do. In Hebrews 12:14 it says, "Follow peace with all men, and holiness, without which no man shall see the Lord:" We see that without "living a holy life" we shall not see the Lord.

We see how God teaches us how His grace causes us to deny ungodliness and worldly lusts.

Titus 2:11-14
11 "For the grace of God that bringeth salvation

What Kind of Attire?

hath appeared to all men,
12 Teaching us that, <u>denying ungodliness and worldly lusts,</u> we should live soberly, righteously, and godly in this present world,
13 Looking for that blessed hope and glorious appearing of our great God and Savior Jesus Christ,
14 Who have Himself for us, that He might redeem us from all iniquity and <u>purify</u> for Himself His own special people, zealous for good works."

Earlier we addressed how bad it is for men to lust after women. Jesus made it very severe for them but like I said, it is not just referring to men, because it says in Matthew 5:27-30 that, "they commit adultery in their heart <u>with her</u>".

I like to compare the lust of men to the lust of women in this way… It is like an electrical outlet… The plug represents a man, the wall receptacle would represent a woman. It takes <u>both</u> to complete the circuit.

We as, women want, (in our human nature), a man to look at us (lust after us) and see us as attractive or beautiful or maybe even seductive. On the opposite side men want to look at women and enjoy/lust after their beauty. So how can we as women blame men for looking or lusting after our bodies if we are by our dress or lack of it, causing /or attracting/seducing men to desire us?

<u>We are just as guilty, according to the Word of God</u>, when we dress in an ungodly seductive manner or acting like the harlots of the world.

I asked my husband, who was in the world for some years, what causes a man to struggle in looking/lusting after a woman. He said clothing that is tight and/or showing the thigh and low-neck exposing cleavage (be aware while bending over) are a temptation and can cause a man to stumble in his walk with the Lord. I know we do not like to feel like we are being legalistic, but there is an answer to that problem also.

Notes:

Notes:

Notes:

"For you, brethren, have been called to liberty; only do not <u>use liberty as an opportunity for the flesh</u>, but through <u>love serve</u> one another."
– Galatians 5:13 NKJV

Chapter Eleven
Liberty in True Beauty

We see in Galatians 5 the issue of legalism being addressed.

I have struggled in this area myself also, wondering if we should even be concerned about how we as, women professing godliness, should dress as long as we are not too extreme in our clothing. But after studying Galatians 5 the Lord seemed to open my eyes to the truth of what is legalism and what is not.

> Galatians 5:1
> *"Stand fast therefore in the liberty wherewith Christ hath made us free, and be not entangled again with the yoke of bondage."*

I used to think that this meant that we should not be too concerned about the outward appearance, of dress or apparel, as long as we were wearing something that was not extreme. But as I said the more I studied this passage in Galatians 5, I could see that Paul was saying that if we are trying to be <u>justified by the law</u> (not from a love relationship with Jesus) we are fallen from grace. (Verses 3 and 4)

I believe that he is talking about circumcision and the laws of the Old Testament. I believe that legalism is trying to obey the Bible in our own strength and in our own flesh. According to the Scriptures and my own experience, when we walk in the Spirit (a close love relationship with Jesus Christ) it is a delight for us to please our Savior and Lord. The commandments that the Word instructs us to do are not grievous but are <u>life and peace to us.</u> (Romans 8:6-9) In 1 John 5:3 we see this… "For this is the love of God, that we keep His commandments: and His commandments <u>are not grievous."</u>

In Galatians 5, we can see that Paul was <u>not</u> talking about our liberty in Christ being to "allow walking in the flesh". In verse 13-14 he makes it very clear…

> *"For, you brethren, have been called to liberty; only do not use <u>liberty as an opportunity for the flesh,</u> but through <u>love serve one another</u>. For all the law is fulfilled in one word, even in this;*

Liberty in True Beauty

You shall love your neighbor as yourself."

(v 16 NKJV)
"I say then: walk in the Spirit, and you shall <u>not</u>
fulfill the <u>lust of the flesh.</u>"

Would you, as a woman professing godliness, say that when a woman dresses in a provocative, attractive or seductive way she is "giving occasion to the flesh"? Do you believe that she is in love serving others? I think not. But if we have an honest and good heart wanting to please the Lord with all of our heart, we will ask God to show us His way of holiness, godliness and righteousness in the area of how we dress and adorn ourselves.

What I have brought out in the Scripture so far is enough to show God's heart in His desire for us to be His temple, glorifying Him in our bodies and spirits. Do you, my dear friend, want to please the Lord in your life by honoring Him with modest, shamefaced, decent, pure apparel and conduct?

From what I read in the Scripture; God is not pleased with anything else. Will we love God and put Him first or love ourselves and put ourselves first?

Notes:

"Oh, worship the Lord in the beauty of holiness: <u>fear</u> before Him, all the earth." – Psalm 96:9

Chapter Twelve
The Beauty of Holiness

This leads me to another subject related to this. Shouldn't we ask ourselves if we are living in the "fear of God"? How important is it to walk in the fear of God? It seems to me that from what I have observed in women is a lack of the fear of God. Do we even understand what the fear of God is?

There is a Scripture in Proverbs 8:13 and that says "The fear of the Lord is to hate evil: pride, and arrogance, and the evil way, and the froward mouth, do I hate." And if our immodest apparel is like a harlot, then isn't it evil and of the evil way?

Do we have pride in our hearts when we are displaying our sexuality to men? It does not sound like having the "fear of God". I believe that the "fear of God" is when we realize that God <u>sees and knows</u> everything. He <u>sees us</u> dressing in a manner that is seductive, attracting men, causing men to lust after us. He knows our heart and motives; so, should we not "fear God"? Maybe many women dress in indecent clothing because they want to be like everyone else, or in other words, not different from the world. But this is also the wrong motive.

In Proverbs we see the following truth.

> *Proverbs 29:25 NKJV*
> *"The fear of man brings a snare: but whoever trusts in the Lord shall be safe."*

If we, as women professing godliness, care more about what other people think about us, than what our God does, then we do have "the fear of man". It says that we cannot fear man and God at the same time, so we have to choose who we will serve.

> *2 Corinthians 6:17-18 NKJV*
> *17 "Therefore, come out from among them, and be separate, says the Lord, Do not touch what is unclean, and I will receive you.*
> *18 I will be a Father to you, and you shall be My sons and daughters, says the Lord Almighty."*

2 Corinthians 7:1 goes on to say, "Having therefore

The Beauty of Holiness

these promises, dearly beloved, let us cleanse ourselves from all <u>filthiness of the flesh</u> and spirit, perfecting holiness <u>in the fear of God</u>."

The real question is do we truly want to fear God which should cause us to cleanse ourselves from all filthiness of the <u>flesh</u> and spirit? Then according to what this passage is saying it sounds like we will have to "come out from among them and be separate and touch not the unclean thing" and that is when God will receive us as His sons and daughters.

This is a truly hard thing for the flesh to submit to God in. We cannot do this in our own selves, we have to cry out for God to help us and to change us. This is not a natural way we as humans are, we want to be accepted by men. Our first and strongest desire should be to "fear God".

If I am reading this passage correctly it seems like it is saying that God does not even receive us as His sons and daughters unless we "come out from among them and be separate".

We see in Matthew 7:13-14 that Jesus said, "Enter you in at the strait gate: for wide is the gate, and broad is the way, that leads to destruction, and many there be which go in there at: Because strait is the gate, and narrow is the way, which leads onto life, and few there be that find it."

We see in verse 21 of the same chapter, it says, "Not everyone that says unto Me, Lord, Lord, shall enter into the kingdom of heaven; but he that does the will of My Father which is in heaven."

What does this say to each and every one of us? Does it sound like it will be easy or that there will be many that will enter into this narrow gate? It says that few will find it. Some may say you are getting into legalism by saying these things. But I am only quoting what the Word of God says to us all.

If we are deceived to think that all we need to do is say a prayer and ask God into our heart and then we just go to Heaven; then, we certainly have not read the Word of God or given heed to it.

> *James 2:19-20*
> *19 "You believe that there is one God. You do well. Even the demons believe—and tremble!*
> *20 But do you want to know, O foolish man, that faith without works is dead?"*

The Beauty of Holiness

In conclusion, my heart, which I feel is God's heart for women, would like to appeal to each and every woman who desires to be a woman professing godliness…

Do you feel that your relationship with Jesus Christ is very personal, very intimate? Are you striving to be pleasing to Him in the way you dress, in everything you do and everything you say? Do you have a very strong desire to be the Bride of Christ?

If so, this is a very life-changing decision that should be contemplated with an honest and good heart. My heart prayer is that every woman would search and seek to be as close and intimate as she can with Jesus, letting Him transform her life and giving her a true UNFADING BEAUTY that shows the joy, peace and lasting love that will reflect God's love to the world.

Notes:

Notes:

In His Presence

By Karen Y. Ranney

Lord Jesus,
In your presence is joy beyond measure,
At your feet I find the greatest treasure.
There is a peace that passes all understanding,
That restores my soul when life is so demanding.
In your presence I feel completely accepted,
By a love that overwhelms my heart and relieves all
that I have dreaded.
In your presence are pleasures forevermore,
Making me look forward to what you have in store…
For me as your bride
In you I want to abide
At your side.
In your presence I feel your gentle embrace,
All my tears are wiped away.
In your presence I know perfect grace
That erases any fears I will face.
Your presence draws me to you, my Beloved,
And I will bask for eternity knowing I am truly loved
In Your Presence.

Song of Solomon 7:10
"I am my beloved's and His desire is towards me."

Dr. Karen Y. Ranney

Adorning Beauty

HOLY
BIBLE
KING JAMES
VERSION

Volume II
Today's Proverb 31 Woman Series

"Look for Book 2, *"Adorning Beauty"* in the Today's Proverb 31 Woman Series that will be coming in the next few months. It is a sequel to the book "Unfading Beauty". It gives more in-depth understanding about how our intimate relationship with Christ will cause us, as women to adorn ourselves with the inner beauty that only Christ can produce in us.

If interested in this volume 2 please email me at: *joyfullynew2015@yahoo.com*

Both Paperback and Kindle ebook are COMING SOON!

I will let you know when they are available.

Would you like to learn more about
Hebraic roots and Messianic ways?
Read this very interesting and enlightening
book about Dr. Karen Y. Ranney's exciting
and joy filled journey learning about God's
Plan for Jew and Gentile alike.

GOD'S PLAN
One New Man

"Will You Be A Part Of It?"

by Dr. Karen Y. Ranney

Ministry Information

Jew and Gentile Ministries is a (501c3) non-profit ministry in the USA. We have a heart for Israel, Jewish people, and the Gentiles to spread the Gospel and Hebraic roots. If you would like us to share with your congregation/church contact us today.

Drs. Allen C. and Karen Y. Ranney can be contacted at:

Jew and Gentile Ministries
P.O. Box 1981, Sapulpa, OK 74066
918-986-4339
www.jewandgentileministries.org
allenranney@yahoo.com

A devoted student of God's Word
Dr. Allen C. Ranney shares in-depth truth that
only time spent with God can reveal.

Using the ancient Torah teaching cycle
(Parashah) as the format, the author
shows/teaches Jesus Christ, Yeshua Messiah,
from the first page of the Bible to the last.

ALL NEW! 5 Volume Set by Dr. Allen C. Ranney

Offered individually in
Paperback and Kindle ebook on
Amazon.com

In this book, the Author sets the record straight about the Church, Isreal, the Jewish people and the great reconciliation miracle God planned from the start.

- Identifying the Olive Tree
- Who is grafted into whom?
- Exposing and avoiding anti-semitism
- God's plan for the Church and Israel remains intact.
- The Lord will reign from Zion.

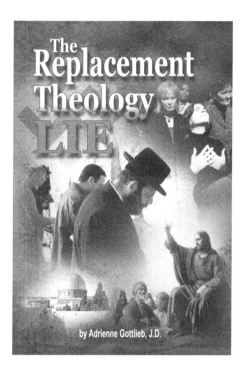

The **Replacement Theology** LIE

by Adrienne Gottlieb, J.D.

"The Church has a tremendous responsibility to be totally committed to the outworking of God's purposes in history." – Adrienne Gottlieb, J.D.

Offered in Paperback and Kindle ebook

Amazon.com

Made in the USA
Columbia, SC
23 October 2020